W9-BMO-877

On the Front Line

FIGHTING THE VIETNAM WAR

Brian Fitzgerald

Chicago, Illinois

Published by Raintree,
a division of Reed Elsevier Inc.
Chicago, IL 60602

Customer Service 888-363-4266
Visit our website at www.heinemannraintree.com

For more information address the publisher:
Raintree, 100 N. LaSalle, Suite 1200, Chicago,
IL 60602

Produced for Raintree Publishers by Discovery Books Ltd
Editorial: Kathryn Walker, Juliet Smith, and Daniel Nunn
Design: Rob Norridge and Michelle Lisseter
Picture Research: Amy Sparks
Project Manager: Juliet Smith
Production: Duncan Gilbert
Printed and bound in China by South China
Printing Company Ltd
Originated by Dot Gradations Ltd

10 09 08 07 06
10 9 8 7 6 5 4 3 2 1

Library of Congress Cataloging-in-Publication Data
Fitzgerald, Brian, 1972-
Fighting the Vietnam war / Brian Fitzgerald.
p. cm. -- (Freestyle express) (On the front line)
Includes index.
ISBN 1-4109-2193-X (lib. bdg) -- ISBN 1-4109-2200-6 (pbk.) 1. Vietnamese Conflict, 1961-1975--Juvenile literature. 2. Vietnamese Conflict, 1961-1975--United States--Juvenile literature. I. Title. II. Series. III. Series: On the front line.

DS557.7.F582 2006
959.704'3--dc22

2005027093

This leveled text is a version of *Freestyle: On the Front Line: Fighting the Vietnam War*

Original edition produced by White-Thomson Publishing Ltd, Bridgewater Business Centre, 210 High Street, Lewes BN7 2NH, United Kingdom.

Acknowledgments
The publishers would like to thank the following for permission to reproduce photographs and maps:
Art Archive pp. 17, 27; AKG p. 22; Alamy p. 32; Camerapress p. 9; Corbis pp. 7, 8, 10, 12, 13, 14, 16(l), 20, 23, 24(l), 25(r), 28, 29, 30, 31, 34–35, 36, 39, 41; Harcourt p. 26; Popperfoto pp. 34(l), 35(r), 38; Topfoto pp. 4–5, 6, 11, 15, 16(r), 18, 19, 21(l), 21(r), 22(l), 24–25, 33, 37, 40.

Cover photograph showing US troops loaded with equipment setting out on a patrol reproduced with permission of AKG.

Map on p. 6 by Peter Bull.

Source notes: pp. 26–27 *The Tunnels of Cu Chi: The Untold Story of Vietnam* by Tom Mangold and John Penycate.

The paper used to print this book comes from sustainable resources.

CONTENTS

Any words appearing in the text in bold, **like this**, are explained in the glossary. You can also look out for them in the Word Bank box at the bottom of each page.

A STRANGE NEW WORLD

A U.S. **marine** sergeant wades through a stream deep in the Vietnamese jungle. He and his men have spent four days searching for enemy troops. Each man is carrying 60 pounds (27 kilograms) of equipment. They are all exhausted.

The soldiers could be surprised by the enemy at any moment. One false move might set off a **booby trap.**

International conflict

During the Vietnam War, the South Vietnamese fought **Communist** troops from the North. Various countries supported South Vietnam. The United States, Australia, South Korea, New Zealand, the Philippines, and Thailand all sent troops to help South Vietnam.

U.S. soldiers needed to stay very alert in Vietnam. Rivers and streams sometimes contained hidden traps.

Word Bank **booby trap** bomb or weapon that is set off when a person touches an object that looks harmless

It is not the type of war the sergeant had been expecting. The battlefields are jungles and small villages. And he still has two more months of **military service** to survive before he can finally go home.

A new enemy

During World War II, the Vietnamese had helped the United States fight Japan. Now the Americans were at war with the Vietnamese. Like millions of others, the soldier wondered, "How did this happen?"

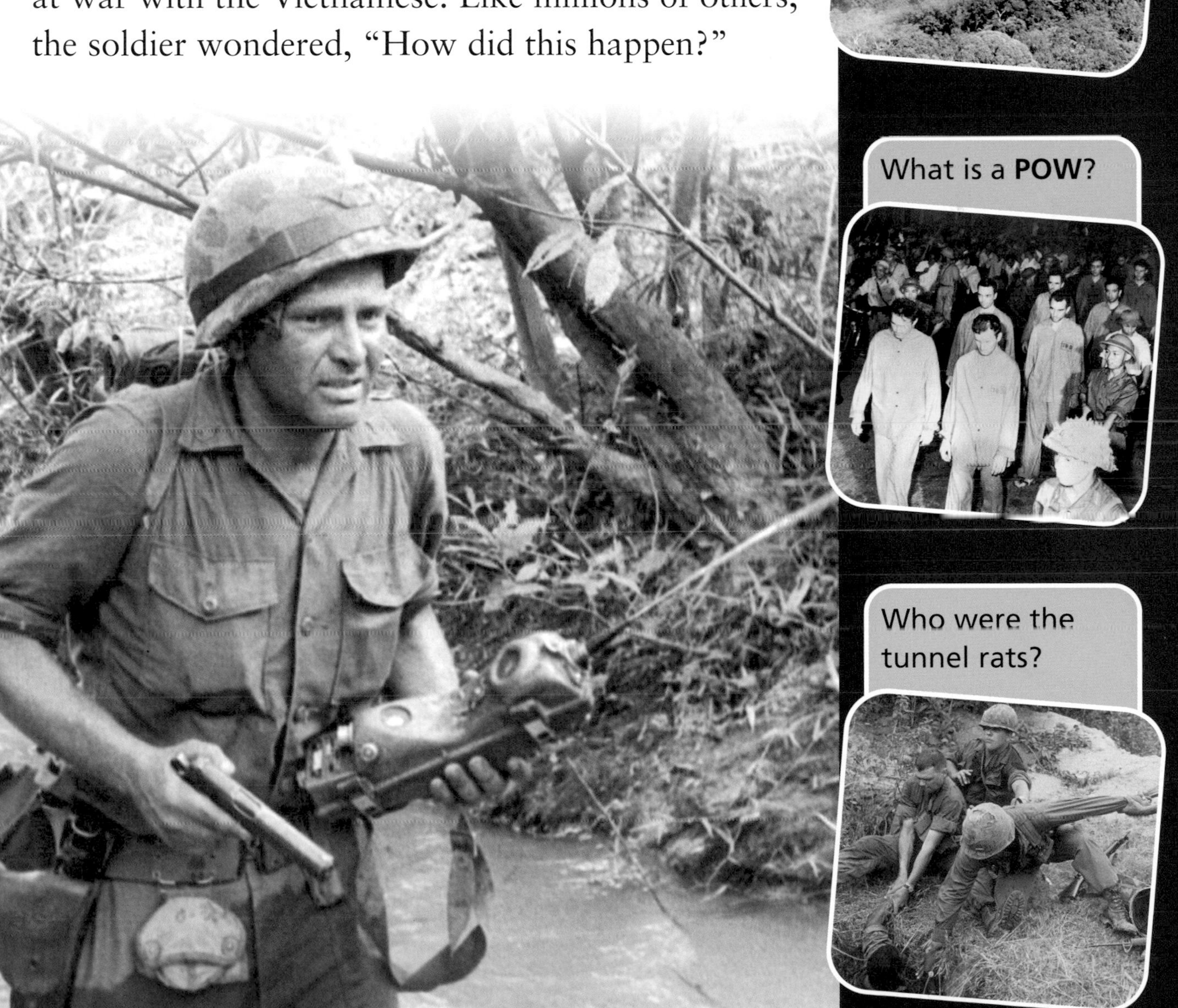

Find out later

What is Agent Orange?

What is a **POW**?

Who were the tunnel rats?

military service time spent working in the armed forces

THE FIRST WAR

In the 1880s the European country of France took control of the Asian countries of Vietnam, Laos, and Cambodia. France named this region French Indochina.

In World War II, Japan invaded Vietnam. Ho Chi Minh was a Vietnamese **Communist** who organized an army to free his country. Ho's army was called

Ho Chi Minh

Ho Chi Minh, pictured below, was a supporter of **Communism**. This is a one-party system of government that puts equality above freedom. He led the fight for Vietnam's independence until he died in 1969.

This map of Vietnam shows some of the key battles of the Vietnam War. It also shows the **Ho Chi Minh Trail** (see page 9).

Word Bank **Communist** someone who supports Communism, a one-party system of government that puts equality above freedom

the **Viet Minh**. They fought the Japanese with U.S. weapons. Japan **surrendered** to the United States in September 1945. World War II came to an end. Ho Chi Minh declared Vietnam a free country.

Fighting the French

The French then tried to take back Vietnam. French troops fought the Viet Minh for nine years. This war ended with a long and bloody battle at Dien Bien Phu in northern Vietnam. On May 7, 1954, the French surrendered.

Support for both sides

When France fought the Vietnamese, both sides received help from other countries. The **Soviet Union** and China sent weapons and money to Ho Chi Minh's communist troops. The United States did not want the Communists to win in Vietnam. It spent more than a billion dollars helping the French.

Vietnamese troops charge up a hill during the battle for Dien Bien Phu.

surrender give yourself up to the enemy

A divided country

In 1954 French troops left Vietnam. A peace agreement was signed. But the **Communists** did not gain immediate control of all Vietnam.

It was decided that national elections would be held in Vietnam in 1956. Until then, the Communists would control North Vietnam. A government that stood against **Communism** would control South Vietnam. Everyone expected the Communists to win the elections in both the North and the South.

A U.S. military adviser trains South Vietnamese troops.

Word Bank Communism one-party system of government that puts equality above freedom

Rebellion in the South

In 1956 the South Vietnamese government refused to hold elections. The United States supported this refusal. In 1959 Communists in the South began a **rebellion** against the South Vietnamese government. The **rebels** soon received help from the North.

These rebels were known as the **Viet Cong.** The Viet Cong had better fighters than the South Vietnamese army. They also had more support. The United States feared the spread of Communism. It sent money, weapons, advisers, and top soldiers to South Vietnam.

Ho Chi Minh Trail

North Vietnam sent help to the Viet Cong in South Vietnam. North Vietnamese moved weapons and supplies to the south along a route known as the **Ho Chi Minh Trail.** The trail is shown on the map on page 6. People either walked or rode bicycles along the trail (see photo on the left).

rebel person who fights against those who are in power

THE UNITED STATES STEPS IN

The **Viet Cong** were **guerrillas**. Guerrillas are soldiers that are not part of a regular army. The Viet Cong fought in small groups. They often used surprise attacks and traps to kill their enemies. The Viet Cong were a powerful enemy.

Top U.S. soldiers known as **Special Forces** were sent to South Vietnam. Their task was to teach the South Vietnamese army how to fight the Viet Cong. But sometimes Special Forces troops found themselves in the middle of the fighting.

South Vietnamese soldiers guard two captured Viet Cong guerrillas. A U.S. soldier watches.

Word Bank **guerrilla** soldier who is not part of a regular army, often fighting as part of a small group

Battle at Nam Dong

On June 6, 1964, the Viet Cong attacked a Special Forces camp at Nam Dong. Nam Dong was in South Vietnam. Captain Roger Donlon rushed to close the main gate. He was shot in the stomach, but kept fighting.

Bravery through pain

Donlon was hit two more times. But this did not stop him from dragging **ammunition** to his men. His courage made his men want to keep going. They defeated the Viet Cong at Nam Dong.

Agent Orange

In 1962 U.S. planes began spraying a chemical over jungles in South Vietnam. The chemical was called Agent Orange. It was used to kill thousands of trees (see picture below). This made it easier to spot the Viet Cong. Agent Orange was later found to cause cancer. It also caused thousands of Vietnamese children to be born with **birth defects**.

ammunition bullets that are fired from a weapon

New president, new plan

On November 22, 1963, U.S. President John F. Kennedy was murdered. Lyndon B. Johnson, the vice president, became president.

President Johnson was worried because the **Viet Cong** were growing stronger. He wanted to send more troops. But he knew most Americans would not want that.

Attack in the Gulf of Tonkin

On August 2, 1964, the warship USS *Maddox* was attacked by North Vietnamese boats in the Gulf of

President Johnson met with his advisers on August 4, 1964, to discuss the crisis in the Gulf of Tonkin.

Word Bank Viet Cong Communist rebels in South Vietnam

Tonkin (see map on page 6). The *Maddox* was supporting South Vietnamese attacks in the Gulf of Tonkin by gathering information. Two days later the *Maddox* and the U.S. warship *C. Turner Joy* reported further attacks.

The president gets new powers

President Johnson claimed these attacks proved that North Vietnam wanted to start a war with the United States. He asked the **U.S. Congress** for powers to do whatever was needed to stop the attacks. Congress agreed to give him the powers.

What really happened?

There is no real proof that the second attack involving the *Maddox* and *C. Turner Joy* (pictured below) happened. The North Vietnamese said they did not fire at the U.S. ships. U.S. crews claimed they had hit at least three enemy boats. But no wreckage or bodies were ever found.

U.S. Congress the highest lawmaking body in the United States

DANGER IN THE AIR

Thunder rolls on

Operation Rolling Thunder was supposed to last a few months. But it lasted more than three years. Many bridges, roads, and buildings were hit. But they were soon repaired. The Ho Chi Minh Trail stayed open. The operation had failed.

President Johnson wanted to end the war quickly. He sent U.S. warplanes to bomb the **Ho Chi Minh Trail** and other important targets in North Vietnam. This operation was called Rolling Thunder.

A dangerous mission

Captain Merlyn Dethlefsen was part of a Rolling Thunder bombing mission. U.S. **bombers** were to be sent to attack an important steel factory in North Vietnam. Dethlefsen's task was to destroy the

Word Bank Ho Chi Minh Trail route along which the North Vietnamese moved supplies to the Viet Cong in South Vietnam

surface-to-air missiles (SAMs) that protected the steel factory.

Mission complete

Dethlefsen flew his fighter plane to the SAM site. But the site was surrounded by **artillery**. Dethlefsen had to dodge fire from the ground and from enemy **fighter planes.**

Dethlefsen's plane was hit. But he kept flying until he had destroyed two missile sites. His bravery allowed U.S. bombers to destroy their targets without losing any planes.

Napalm strike

Some U.S. planes dropped **napalm**. Napalm was a sticky gel that burst into flames when it hit the air. It was meant to destroy enemy targets, but it also burned thousands of **civilians**. The child in this picture was badly burned by napalm.

◄ A flight of three fighter planes refuel in the air on their way to bomb targets in North Vietnam in 1966.

surface-to-air missile (SAM) missile launched from the ground to destroy enemy aircraft

Shot down over Hanoi

In October 1967 U.S. pilot John McCain took off on a bombing raid. His target was Hanoi, the capital of North Vietnam. He did not return for five years.

McCain's plane was shot down. McCain ejected from his plane but broke one knee and both his arms. He was captured and became a **prisoner of war (POW)**.

John McCain (bottom right) poses with other U.S. Navy pilots in 1965.

These captured U.S. pilots were forced to march through the streets of Hanoi.

Word Bank prisoner of war (POW) soldier who is captured and put in prison by the enemy during a war

Prisoner of war

McCain lay in an empty cell for four days before he was taken to the hospital. There a doctor fixed only one of his arms. He waited more than a month for an operation on his knee.

McCain was beaten and **tortured.** But he refused to give information to the North Vietnamese. He was not allowed to see or talk to other prisoners for two years. He was released in 1973.

John McCain is a U.S. senator today. He represents Arizona in the U.S. Senate in Washington, DC.

POWs and MIAs

- North Vietnam released 802 prisoners at the end of the war.
- 661 of these were U.S. military men. Nearly 500 were pilots who had been shot down.
- 2,583 U.S. military men were listed as **"missing in action"** (MIA).

This North Vietnamese poster calls the United States a "paper tiger." This term suggested that the United States was not as powerful as it seemed. The **Communists** used anti-United States posters like this one to try to win new supporters in South Vietnam.

missing in action (MIA) term used to describe a soldier who does not return from a war and whose body is never found

LOOKING FOR A HIDDEN ENEMY

The draft

Many U.S. troops were needed for the "search and destroy" plan. Men between 18 and 25 were **drafted**. This meant they were ordered by law to join the armed forces. More than two million Americans were drafted for the war.

The first U.S. ground troops arrived in Vietnam in March 1965. At first, their job was to protect positions in the south. But this soon changed.

"Search and destroy"

Soldiers from the North Vietnamese army were now supporting the **Viet Cong** in the south. The South Vietnamese army alone could not stop its enemies from taking control. The United States decided to use its troops to help. The troops were to search out and destroy the enemy.

U.S. soldiers sometimes burned down Vietnamese villages during "search and destroy" missions. They did this if they suspected the villagers were helping the Viet Cong.

Word Bank Viet Cong Communist rebels in South Vietnam

Early clash

U.S. troops faced the North Vietnamese army for the first time at the Battle of Ia Drang. It was November 1965. The Ia Drang Valley was in South Vietnam. The North Vietnamese army had the most men. But the United States troops had **bombers** and helicopters.

The United States won. The North Vietnamese could not match U.S. equipment. They realized that the best way to fight the United States was with **guerrilla warfare** (see page 10).

Help from Australia

The United States was not the only country that sent soldiers to South Vietnam. South Korea and Australia also sent troops. Australia and the United States sometimes worked together on secret missions.

An Australian soldier wearing a jungle "boonie" hat takes cover behind a tree.

guerrilla warfare fighting with small groups of soldiers who hide and make sudden attacks on the enemy

Help from above

Helicopters were very important in the Vietnam War. Soldiers called them "Hueys" or "choppers." They were used to carry troops in and out of dangerous areas.

During the battle of Ia Drang, U.S. soldiers were surrounded by North Vietnamese troops. The Americans were running out of **ammunition**. But their commander would not let helicopters

Life savers

Helicopters saved many lives in Vietnam. They landed in dangerous areas to take the injured to hospitals. Many chopper crews were killed or injured trying to rescue others.

U.S. troops jump from a Huey into battle.

Word Bank **ammunition** bullets that are fired from a weapon

land because it was too dangerous. One pilot decided to land his helicopter anyway.

A heroic pilot

Captain Ed Freeman's helicopter was not armed with weapons. But Freeman made many trips through heavy gunfire to the troops. He took them ammunition, water, and medical supplies. Freeman and his crew also flew more than 30 injured men to safety.

Mail call

Choppers brought supplies to soldiers. Some soldiers say the most important delivery was the mail. Soldiers in Vietnam had no other contact with family or friends.

An injured U.S. soldier is carried to a helicopter.

Trouble in the jungle

The search and destroy missions led U.S. troops into the Vietnamese jungle. Small groups of U.S. soldiers moved through mud and **rice paddies**. They had to be very careful of **booby traps**. A **trip wire** could set off a hidden bomb.

Each man carried all his equipment on his back. His pack could weigh up to 70 pounds (32 kilograms). When soldiers sat down, the

Booby traps

Soldiers needed to watch out for booby traps such as:

- Toe poppers—bullets placed on sharp bamboo sticks. The bullets fired when stepped on.
- Punji stakes—sharp bamboo sticks in a small hole, covered with leaves.

U.S. troops, loaded with gear, set out on a **patrol**.

Word Bank rice paddy area where rice is grown

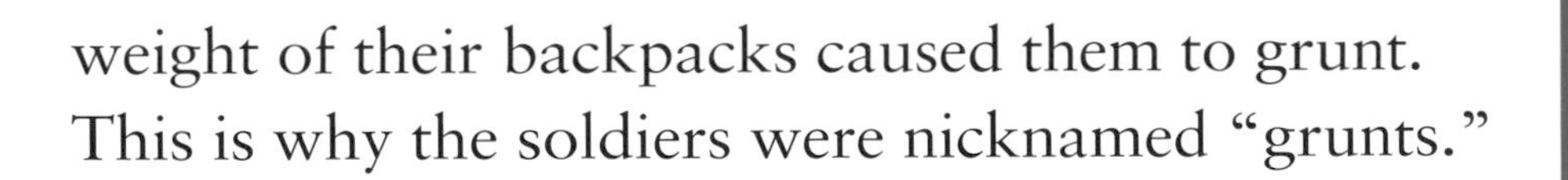

weight of their backpacks caused them to grunt. This is why the soldiers were nicknamed "grunts."

Invisible enemy

The **Viet Cong** often hid in the thick jungle. They would attack without warning. Grunts knew the Viet Cong often attacked at night. Because of this, grunts did not get much sleep.

It was often hard for the U.S. soldiers to see their enemy. The Viet Cong did not wear uniforms. It was difficult to tell an innocent farmer from an enemy soldier.

A grunt takes a break from patrol to eat. Soldiers carried their food in their backpacks.

trip wire wire stretched close to the ground that sets off an explosion when touched

Trouble in the water

Small U.S. Navy boats **patrolled** the Mekong River delta in South Vietnam. They were called swift boats. The Americans wanted to keep weapons from getting to the **Viet Cong** by river. They also wanted to search for Viet Cong who hid along the waterway.

John Kerry was in charge of a swift boat. One night in 1965, Kerry and his crew rushed to help another boat under attack. A rocket exploded near

R and R

After patrols soldiers sometimes had a few days of rest and relaxation (called "R and R"). Some soldiers went to camps with beautiful beaches, as shown in the photograph below.

Word Bank patrol search for enemy troops

Kerry's boat. Kerry jumped ashore and saw a Viet Cong soldier with a **rocket launcher**. Kerry killed the soldier before he could fire at his boat.

Heroic action

Four months later a **mine** blew up near Kerry's boat. One of his men fell overboard. The enemy soldiers were firing at the man in the water. Kerry's arm was bleeding, and he was in great pain. But he still managed to pull the man out of the water.

Bravery rewarded

John Kerry was awarded medals for his bravery in Vietnam. But he later became a **protester** against the war. The picture below shows Kerry speaking out against the war on television. In 2004 Kerry ran in the election for president of the United States. He was beaten by George W. Bush.

Three U.S. patrol boats cruise the Mekong River in search of Viet Cong **guerrillas**.

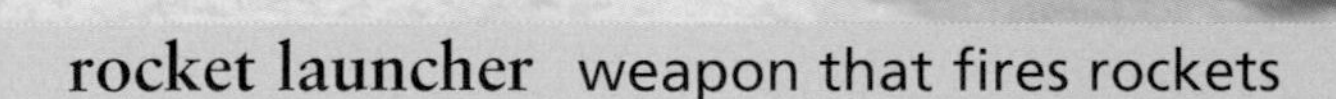

rocket launcher weapon that fires rockets

The underground world

The **Viet Cong** built a series of tunnels in South Vietnam. They used them to hide from the U.S. troops. They also used them to shelter from bombs.

Hospital under threat

Viet Cong doctor Vo Hoang Le worked in an unusual hospital. It was 15 feet (5 meters) under the ground! Some of his surgical instruments were made from parts of shot-down U.S. planes and helicopters.

The Viet Cong used underground cities such as this one to hide from U.S. attacks.

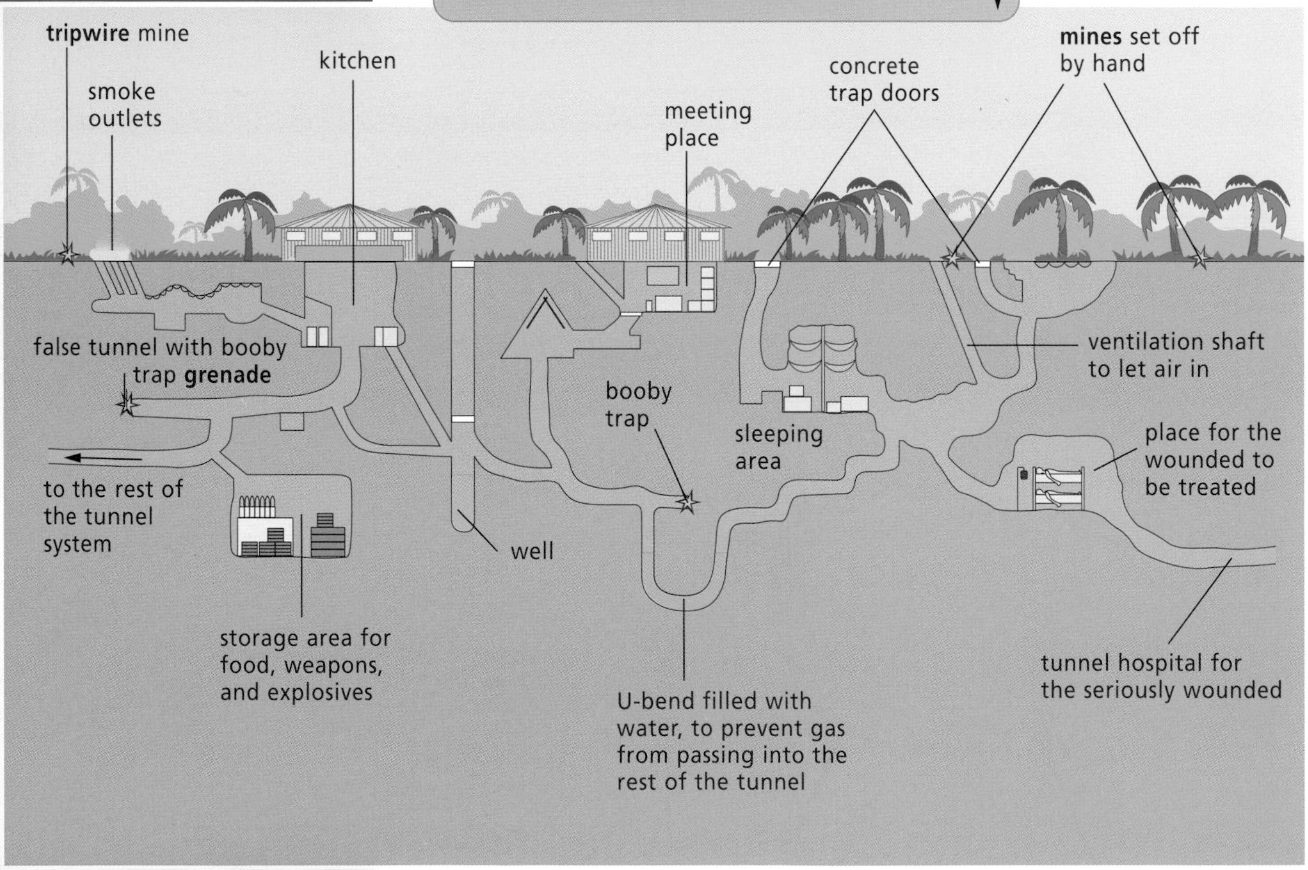

tripwire mine
smoke outlets
kitchen
meeting place
concrete trap doors
mines set off by hand
false tunnel with booby trap **grenade**
ventilation shaft to let air in
booby trap
sleeping area
place for the wounded to be treated
to the rest of the tunnel system
well
storage area for food, weapons, and explosives
U-bend filled with water, to prevent gas from passing into the rest of the tunnel
tunnel hospital for the seriously wounded

Word Bank Viet Cong Communist rebels in South Vietnam

One day, U.S. soldiers were moving toward the tunnel that led to the hospital. Le had to protect his 60 patients. He hid in a small hole covered with leaves. When the soldiers moved closer, he fired his gun. All three soldiers fell to the ground.

A determined doctor

A few months later, Le was shot in the right hand. He was no longer able to use it. Instead, he taught himself to perform surgery using his left hand.

Tunnel rats

The U.S. soldiers who explored the Viet Cong tunnels were known as tunnel rats. They faced many dangers. These included **booby traps**, snakes, and being shot at by Viet Cong soldiers.

This soldier is being lowered into a tunnel as part of a search and destroy mission.

booby trap bomb or weapon that is set off when a person touches an object that looks harmless

THE TIDE TURNS

In January 1968 both sides agreed to stop fighting for a few days. This would allow Vietnamese soldiers on both sides to celebrate the New Year. The Vietnamese New Year is called "Tet."

The Tet Offensive

On January 30 Viet Cong and North Vietnamese troops broke this agreement. They made a surprise attack on more than 100 South Vietnamese towns and cities. Saigon was one of the cities they attacked. This attack is known as the Tet Offensive.

U.S. troops try to take control of the streets of Saigon after the Tet Offensive of 1968.

Word Bank marine soldier that serves at sea and on land

The U.S. military quickly recovered from the surprise attack. It took them just a few days to take back most of South Vietnam.

Communist defeat

The **Communists** had failed to take South Vietnam. They had hoped that the South Vietnamese would rise up against the southern government. This did not happen. The Communists lost ten times as many men as the United States and South Vietnamese armies.

U.S. **marines** fire a machine gun at North Vietnamese troops during the battle at Khe Sanh.

A long siege

About a week before Tet, the North Vietnamese attacked a U.S. base at Khe Sanh. It was not a very important base. But the United States refused to let it go. The **siege** of Khe Sanh lasted 77 days. Finally, the North Vietnamese soldiers were forced back.

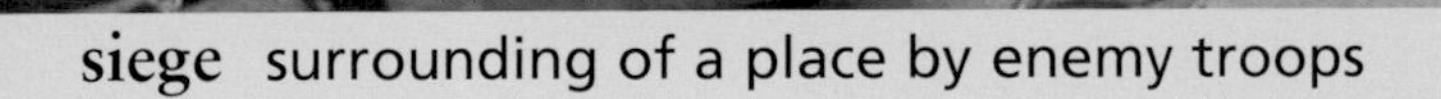

siege surrounding of a place by enemy troops

A losing victory

The Tet Offensive ended in victory for the United States. But it had shown that the **Communists** were still very powerful. Many people now thought the United States could not win the war.

A TV war

The Vietnam War was called the first television war. The American people saw the horror of war each night on the news. They saw troops killed and towns destroyed by bombs. Television news reports turned some people against the war.

Protests

Since 1965 **protests** against the war had been taking place in the United States. Many Americans thought their country should not be fighting the Vietnam War. They felt it was wrong because Vietnam was not a threat to the United States.

Images such as this one of three wounded U.S. soldiers were very common during the Vietnam War.

Word Bank **protest** showing disapproval of something. Protests often take the form of marches or public gatherings.

After the Tet Offensive, more joined the protests. They included people who had fought in Vietnam. Many young men refused to go to war. Some went to live in Canada or Europe to avoid being **drafted**.

New leader

In 1968 the United States had to elect a new president. President Johnson did not want to be re-elected. Another president would have to find a way to end the war.

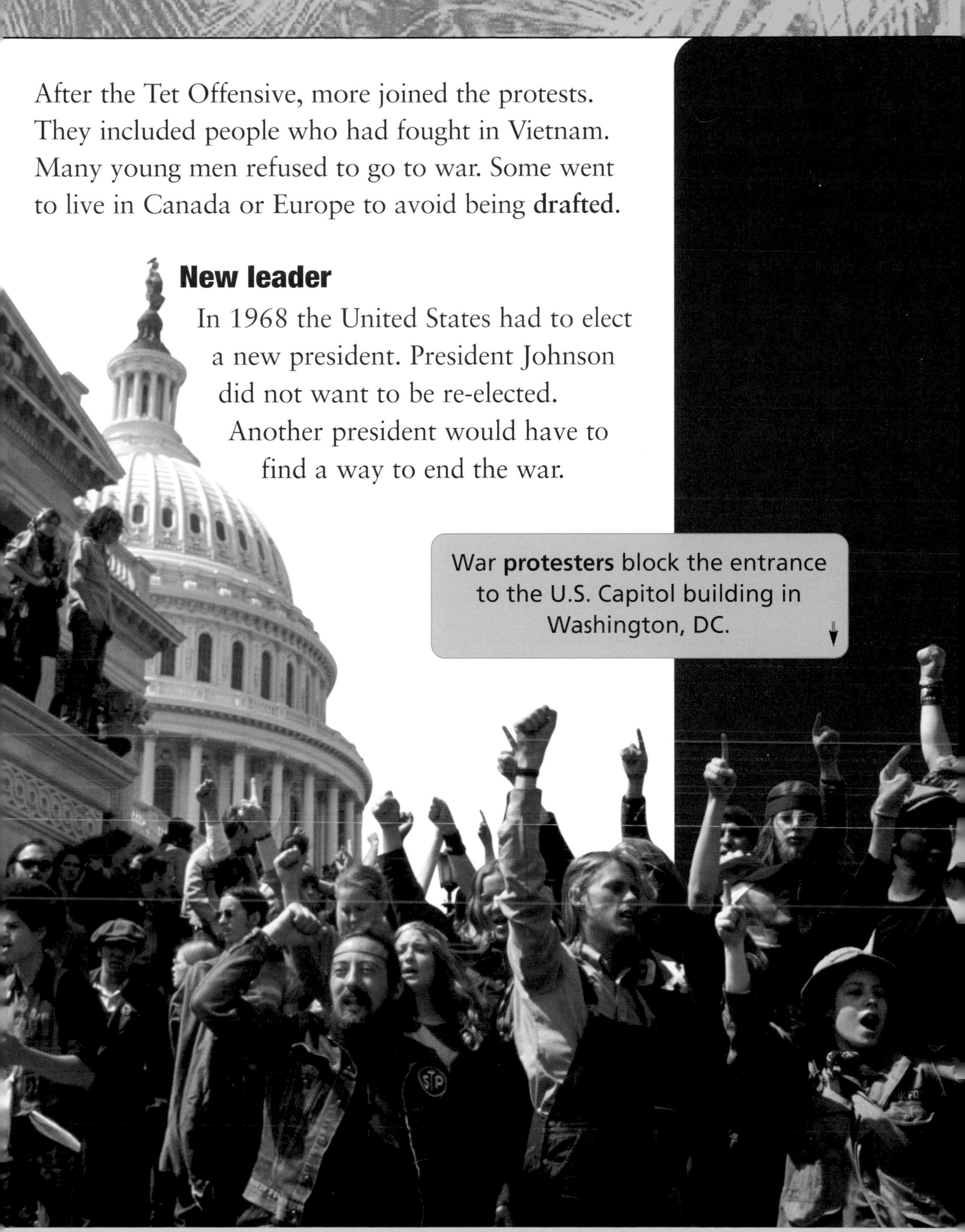

War **protesters** block the entrance to the U.S. Capitol building in Washington, DC.

protester person who shows disagreement by joining a march or by refusing to do something

A PROMISE OF PEACE

Richard Nixon was elected president of the United States in November 1968. He said he had a plan for ending the war, not winning it.

The plan

Nixon's plan was that the South Vietnamese army would take over most of the fighting. They would be trained by U.S. troops and use U.S. weapons. Then the Americans could go home.

Army drug abuse

Many soldiers used illegal drugs in Vietnam. More than half of the U.S. troops smoked marijuana (a drug made from the hemp plant). Some of those who used even more dangerous drugs became **addicts**.

Many U.S. soldiers wanted peace in Vietnam just as much as people back in the United States.

Word Bank addict person who cannot stop doing or using something

There were problems with this plan. The South Vietnamese army was in bad shape. The soldiers were used to having U.S. troops fight for them. Many South Vietnamese troops **deserted**.

Soldiers want out

Nixon's plan also had a bad effect on U.S. troops. Their aim had been to win the war. Now they just wanted to get out alive. Some soldiers refused to obey orders to fight. Some even deserted.

Hamburger Hill

The battle for Hamburger Hill took place in May 1969. Hamburger Hill was on South Vietnam's northern border. Seventy U.S. soldiers died in the battle. Shortly after taking the hill, the army abandoned it. It seemed to many that the bloodshed had been pointless.

U.S. troops rush a wounded soldier to a helicopter during the battle for Hamburger Hill.

deserted left without permission

More problems for Nixon

In 1969 President Nixon faced a new problem back home. In November 1969 the public heard about a horrible event. The event had been kept secret for more than a year.

The secret

In 1968 a group of U.S. soldiers had arrived in a village called My Lai in South Vietnam. The men had

Vietnamese **civilians** often found themselves in the line of fire. Here, an elderly woman and her grandchild take cover in a field.

Word Bank civilian someone who is not in the armed forces

been told that the **Viet Cong** were in the area. They wanted revenge for friends killed by the Viet Cong.

Innocent victims

But in the village, the U.S. troops found only women, children, and old men. They took out their anger on the helpless villagers. The soldiers murdered about 500 innocent people.

When Americans at home heard about My Lai, they became angry. They felt the government had lied to them. They were even angrier that U.S. troops would commit such an awful crime.

Student deaths

On May 4, 1970, U.S. troops were called to break up a **protest** at Kent State University, Ohio. The troops used **tear gas**, but the **protesters** did not leave (see photograph below). Then the troops shot at the students. Four students died, and nine were injured. The violence shocked the world.

This elderly South Vietnamese man is being led away by a U.S. soldier. The soldier suspected him of supporting the Viet Cong.

tear gas type of gas that makes the eyes fill with tears

THE UNITED STATES PULLS OUT

Peace talks between the United States and North Vietnam began in 1968. The talks dragged on for years. In 1972 an agreement was almost reached. But then the peace talks broke down.

The Christmas bombings

On December 18, 1972, President Nixon ordered a massive bombing attack on Hanoi. Hanoi was North Vietnam's capital. The attack lasted twelve days and became known as the "Christmas bombings."

The Christmas bombings left much of Hanoi in ruins.

Word Bank prisoner of war (POW) soldier who is captured and put in prison by the enemy during a war

Thousands of civilians were killed, but the North Vietnamese refused to change their demands. The United States decided to accept their terms. South Vietnam had no choice but to agree as well.

Good-bye Vietnam

U.S. troops left Vietnam in March 1973. More than 58,000 Americans had been killed. About 300,000 had been wounded. Billions of dollars had been spent. Nothing had been gained. The South Vietnamese were now left to fight alone.

Peace details

The 1973 peace agreement stated:

- there would be an end to fighting in Vietnam
- armies on both sides would keep whatever land they held
- U.S. troops would leave Vietnam within 60 days
- all **prisoners of war** would be returned

A former U.S. prisoner of war is reunited with his family in March 1973.

Fighting begins again

North and South Vietnam soon broke the peace agreement. Both sides again fought for control of South Vietnam.

South Vietnam was no longer protected by U.S. troops. The South Vietnamese army was running out of supplies. Things looked bad for them.

Broken promise

The United States had promised to help South Vietnam if the **Communists** broke the peace agreement. But it did nothing. U.S. leaders were no longer interested in this unpopular war.

Operation Frequent Wind

The day before Saigon was captured, the United States sent rescue helicopters into the city. These helicopters picked up U.S. citizens and many South Vietnamese. In the photograph on the right, people are desperately trying to board a helicopter. They are trying to get out of Saigon before North Vietnamese troops capture the city.

Word Bank **Communist** someone who supports Communism, a one-party system of government that puts equality above freedom

One last attack

In early 1975, the Communists quickly moved through many South Vietnamese cities. By the middle of April, the North Vietnamese army surrounded Saigon.

Saigon falls

On April 30, 1975, North Vietnamese army tanks and trucks rolled into Saigon. The South Vietnamese president surrendered. The Communists renamed the capital Ho Chi Minh City. They named it after their great leader who had died in 1969.

North Vietnamese troops proudly show their flag. They have captured the presidential palace in Saigon.

Boat people

Some Vietnamese no longer wanted to live in their homeland. Many escaped from Vietnam on boats. More than one million of these "boat people" settled in the United States alone.

Trying to forget

The United States had never lost a war until Vietnam. It was the longest war Americans had ever fought. Many Americans wanted to forget about Vietnam.

This photograph was taken in Saigon in the final days of the war. These people are leaving Vietnam in the hope of making a better life elsewhere. ↓

Word Bank veteran person who served in the armed forces

To some Americans, this meant forgetting the men who had fought bravely in Vietnam. These men were not treated like the heroes of past wars. Many could not return to normal life. They could not forget the horror of the war.

Vietnam's suffering

War left much of Vietnam in ruins. As many as three million Vietnamese people may have died during the fighting.

U.S. Memorial

In 1982 the Vietnam **Veterans'** Memorial in Washington, DC, was completed. The long stone wall lists the names of more than 58,000 soldiers who died or remain missing in Vietnam. The memorial aims to make sure that the soldiers who died in Vietnam will not be forgotten.

TIME LINE

1945		
September 2	Ho Chi Minh declares Vietnam is free from France. Both sides go to war.
1954	
May 7	The French **surrender** at Dien Bien Phu.
July 21	At the Geneva Peace Conference, it is decided that national elections will be held in Vietnam in 1956. The country is divided into North Vietnam and South Vietnam until then.
1956	The president of South Vietnam refuses to hold elections. He is supported by the United States.
1959	**Communists** in South Vietnam—the **Viet Cong**—begin a **rebellion** against the South Vietnamese government. The Viet Cong are supported by North Vietnam.
1964	
August 2	The USS *Maddox* is attacked by North Vietnamese boats in the Gulf of Tonkin.
1965	
March 2	The U.S. Rolling Thunder bombing operation begins.
March 8	The first U.S. **combat** troops arrive in South Vietnam.
Oct.–Nov.	The Battle of Ia Drang is fought.
1968	
January 21	The **siege** of Khe Sanh begins.
January 30	The Tet Offensive begins.

March 16 U.S. troops attack the village of My Lai, killing hundreds of **civilians**.

1969

May 20 The ten-day battle for Hamburger Hill ends.

June 8 U.S. President Nixon announces the first withdrawals of U.S. troops from Vietnam.

November 15 More than 250,000 people take part in an antiwar **protest** in Washington, DC.

1970

May 4 Four students protesting at Kent State University in Ohio are killed by National Guard troops.

1971

August 18 Australia announces the withdrawal of its troops from South Vietnam.

1972

December 18 The Christmas bombings of Hanoi by the United States begin.

1973

January 27 A peace agreement is signed in Paris, France.

February 12 The first group of U.S. **prisoners of war** is released from North Vietnam.

March 29 The last U.S. combat troops leave Vietnam.

1975

April 30 North Vietnamese troops take Saigon.

FIND OUT MORE

Organizations

National Vietnam Veterans' Art Museum

This museum houses works of art on the subject of the Vietnam War. All works are created by artists who served in the war. The collection includes paintings, sculpture, photographs, music, and poetry.

You can contact the museum at the following address:

1801 S. Indiana Avenue
Chicago,
IL 60616

Books

Gifford, Clive. *Vietnam War (How Did It Happen?)*. San Diego: Lucent Books, 2005.

Murray, Stuart. *Eyewitness: Vietnam War (Eyewitness Books)*. New York: Dorling Kindersley Publishing, 2004.

Myers, Walter Dean. *Patrol: An American Soldier in Vietnam*. New York: Harper Collins, 2001.

DVD/VHS

These DVDs and VHS contain upsetting images of war. Ask a parent or teacher before watching these.

Vietnam: A Television History (1983)
This thirteen-part series looks at Vietnam's struggle for freedom and how it affected people on both sides of the fighting. Note: The 2004 DVD release includes only eleven parts of the original thirteen-part series.

Vietnam War with Walter Cronkite (DVD 2003)
A three-part series that includes interviews and film of the war that have never been seen before.

World Wide Web

To find out more about the Vietnam War, you can search the Internet. Use keywords such as these:

- "Operation Rolling Thunder"
- Vietnam + protest
- U.S. troops + Vietnam

You can find your own keywords by using words from this book. The search tips below will help you find useful Web sites.

Most Web sites are aimed at adults. They can contain upsetting information and pictures. Make sure that you use well-known sites with correct information.

Search tips

There are billions of pages on the Internet. It can be difficult to find exactly what you are looking for. These tips will help you find useful Web sites more quickly:

- Know what you want to find out about.
- Use simple keywords.
- Use two to six keywords in a search.
- Only use names of people, places, or things.
- Put double quotation marks around words that go together, for example, "Ho Chi Minh Trail."

Where to search

Search engine

A search engine looks through millions of Web site pages. It lists all the sites that match the words in the search box. You will find the best matches are at the top of the list on the first page.

Search directory

A person instead of a computer has sorted a search directory. You can search by keyword or subject and browse through the different sites. It is like looking through books on a library shelf.

GLOSSARY

addict person who cannot stop doing or using something

ammunition bullets that are fired from a weapon

artillery large mounted guns that fire shells or missiles

birth defect something wrong in a baby that develops either before birth or at the time of birth

bomber aircraft designed to carry and drop bombs

booby trap bomb or weapon that is set off when a person touches an object that looks harmless

civilian someone who is not in the armed forces

combat fighting

Communism one-party system of government that puts equality above freedom

Communist someone who supports Communism, a one-party system of government that puts equality above freedom

deserted left without permission

draft order to do military service

fighter plane fast aircraft designed to fight and destroy enemy aircraft

grenade weapon filled with explosives

guerrilla soldier who is not part of a regular army, often fighting as part of a small group

guerrilla warfare fighting with small groups of soldiers who hide and make sudden attacks on the enemy

Ho Chi Minh Trail route along which the North Vietnamese moved supplies to the Viet Cong in South Vietnam

marine soldier that serves at sea and on land

military service time spent working in the armed forces

mine type of bomb put in the sea or under soil

missing in action (MIA) term used to describe a soldier who does not return from a war and whose body is never found

napalm sticky gel made from gasoline that bursts into flames when it hits the air

patrol search for enemy troops

prisoner of war (POW) soldier who is captured and put in prison by the enemy during a war

protest showing disapproval of something. Protests often take the form of marches or public gatherings.

protester person who shows disagreement by joining a march or by refusing to do something

rebel person who fights against those who are in power

rebellion when a group of people join together to fight against the people who are in power

rice paddy area where rice is grown

rocket launcher weapon that fires rockets

siege surrounding of a place by enemy troops

Soviet Union country that once spread across northern Asia into Eastern Europe and included what is now Russia

Special Forces top soldiers in the U.S. Army

surface-to-air missile (SAM) missile launched from the ground to destroy enemy aircraft

surrender give yourself up to the enemy

tear gas type of gas that makes the eyes fill with tears

tortured beaten or forced to suffer pain. Torture is sometimes used on prisoners to get secret information from them.

trip wire wire stretched close to the ground that sets off an explosion when touched

U.S. Congress the highest lawmaking body in the United States

veteran person who served in the armed forces

Viet Cong Communist rebels in South Vietnam

Viet Minh Vietnamese armed forces led by Ho Chi Minh that defeated the Japanese and later the French in Vietnam

INDEX